GW00633148

Golden Reflections

The Heavenly Brew

Fur of a fluffy rabbit
In the pot you must lay it,
Feather of bird and paw of cat,
The softness of a welcome mat,
Robin's chest and angel's wings,
The 'dawn chorus' songbirds sing,
For a charm of divine flings,
In the pot you must put these things.

———————

Double, double gentle and kind,
In the pot you must stir, not grind!

Ben Yeardye
(aged 13)

Golden Reflections

Julia Eva Yeardye

N´ee Julie (Jewel) Wright

(Dedicated to our grandchildren)

First published in February 2005 by:
Julia Eva Yeardye

ISBN:
0-9543766-1-7

Printed and bound in Great Britain by:
ProPrint
Riverside Cottages
Old Great North Road
Stibbington
Cambridgeshire
PE8 6LR

Foreword

On the afternoon of Sunday, 11th May, 2003, some of us walked the boundaries of the Parish of Hawridge, in Buckinghamshire. It was, after all, an ancient Rogationtide custom and some of our number had done it often. Some of us had not but, after all, what was eight miles to those of us who were at our peak of fitness – or just a little past it?

The walk took us through beautiful scenery, wonderful views, through valleys and along the top of ridges, but, for some of us at least, the last few miles were the longest, and aching limbs, sore feet and the welcome cup of tea at the end could have been the most enduring memories eclipsing the beauty of the countryside.

Except that, fortunately, we had a poet with us, in whom the beauty of the countryside through which we passed, was able to sink deeply, to emerge a very few days later as 'The Bluebell Wood'.

I am grateful to Julia for this memorial of that day, which takes me back to the companionship and enjoyment of the walk more surely, and eloquently, than my own memories do.

Julia's poems cover a wide range of human experience. There is satire, as in 'Melanie's Menagerie – at Hitcham' and 'Winter's Chill', the patriotism of 'This Fair Land of Ours – England', which is reflected in many of her other poems also.

The very personal test of faith shown in 'He Has Given Me Strength', in which Julia shows us something of her personal struggle and her deep faith in God, as well as the apparently prosaic experience, (which surely no one could find poetic!) of being at 'The Surgery'. But the poet can find depths in that, which to the rest of us, is meaningless and so ordinary!

For those of us who do not have Julia's way with words, there is that encouragement to look at things more deeply, to be more thoughtful and find deeper significance in our experiences, in a world in which we are encouraged to live in a shallow and superficial way – in a word, to be more contemplative.

Rev. Ivor Cornish,
Curate of Hawridge, with Cholesbury and
St. Leonards, and of The Lee

Contents

Forge a Path Ahead

Altho' you know there is so much opposition,
  To the plans that you have both made,
Knowing your own mind, act on your own volition
  And dispel those fears, your worries allayed,
Send them on their way, you have a will of your own,
  The die is cast, your hope-seeds long ago sown.

Sitting around, feeling sorry, takes you nowhere at all,
  But take care, for you can so easily be led astray,
The evil intentions of others can take many forms, to appal,
  And you may, from your chosen goal, be driven away,
Just when you had reached a decision to forge ahead,
  Another angry soul can fill you with dread.

Many others may try to dissuade and turn you away,
  But stick to those principles, stay on the path,
You may need help along the way, 'no man an island' obey,
  When you meet with derision, force a laugh,
Keep on smiling as you stride on boldly ahead,
  Then you might find to your aim you are led.

Wise ones say, "Above all, to thine own self be true",
  Seek genuine help and no shame that you ask,
Show you can make it and others will believe in you too,
  True friends will support and share your task,
As for the others, they are worthless anyway, but only you,
  With grim determination, can prove your colours true.

It will not be easy, but you are not entirely alone,
  Though you need to come down to earth again,
And settle patiently for brighter prospects to condone,
  Keep on believing that you will come thro' the rain,
So that whatever you do, wherever you may tread,
  You can find a way – and forge that path ahead.

Bravery Through Fear
(For My Brother)

What traumas distract and upset your mind,
    Yet they had to be cruel, to be kind.
When you were told of your worst fears,
    Did you travel back over all the years
To those favoured places and boyhood haunts,
    Where, with pals, you had enjoyed many jaunts,
Knowing you would never see their like again,
    And will the mem'ries bring joy or pain?
You needed to find a bravado unknown, till now,
    To wrestle with thoughts and a worried brow,
        Yet bravery is near, to follow fear.

It has taken its toll, coming to terms
    With your illness deepset, terminal, affirmed,
But now you know and will put up a fight,
    You might even put this bogey to flight.
Your greatest hope, to make it all go away,
    With a God-given chance, to live another day,
Then pray to Him, with all might and main,
    That He will guide and keep you from pain,
Will nurture your strength, give His strong arm
    And lead you away from a self-inflicted harm,
        Sheer bravery near, to counteract fear.

Family and friends with you each step of the way,
    Giving assurance to you, they constantly pray
As you struggle to overcome foreboding and fear,
    But find it too hard to recall yesteryear,
When you were so young, so strong and able
    And life seemed more consistent and stable.
Now old age, interminable aches and pains,
    Adding to your torment, uncertainty – disdains
Your unhappy circumstance, ever-present ills,
    Putting to flight treasured boyhood ideals,
        Yet remain brave tho' your plight be grave.

Altho' deep down you know your indulgence kills,
Even as you swallow life's bitterest pills,
Remember that bravery can always conquer fear
And that His strong arm is ever near.

* * *

The Sweetness of a Rose

Masses of flowers may well-perform – in contrast to the rose,
But she stands tallest of all in her own bed,
Her colour and grace divine – in so glorious a pose,
Giving her all to those about to wed.

Her heady perfumes add to her perfection so pure,
And she can charm to sweetest delight,
For no other bloom can match her allure,
Her winning ways bewitch us, our senses incite.

When you enter a room you know she is there,
Ever-gracious, in sweet repose, to entice and intoxicate all,
She will fascinate guests with a seductive air,
Enchanting, till under her spell they fall,
So precocious is Madame Rose,
That she can lead them by the nose!

It Costs Nothing to Smile

When the everyday worries of life bring pain,
    And those heaven sent opportunities are slain,
By wearing a smile you can conquer every ill,
    And find, after all, you possess a stronger will.
        To send your gremlins on their way –
        And discover some peace at the end of day.

How strange it feels to send a smile across a room,
    When your recipient merely turns aside with gloom,
Little did he know the dagger-thrust to your heart,
    For, after all, he could easily have played a part,
        Could it be he's should 'ring worries of his own?
        Just forgive him and stifle that moan.

How many people we meet along life's road,
    Who never strive to rise above their heavy load,
Who would rather grizzle and get everyone down
    And carry their burdens all alone, wearing a frown.
        But keep trying, in the end they may give in,
        When they see, in spite of self-doubt, a happy grin!

Why is it that some folk find it hard to smile?
    Rather than force one they'd sooner run a mile,
You long to say, 'When life seems grey, don't turn away,
    Find someone who can listen while you may
        And remember always, it costs nothing to smile,
        Wearing one could make life more worthwhile.'

And those heavy loads will seem far lighter,
    Your day, your whole life will appear brighter,
When you share, with others, your pain and grief,
    No one but you can feel the utter relief.
        So when the day seems long, strike up in song,
        Wearing a dazzling smile the whole day long!

LOOKS LIKE
IT WILL
TIP
OVER..

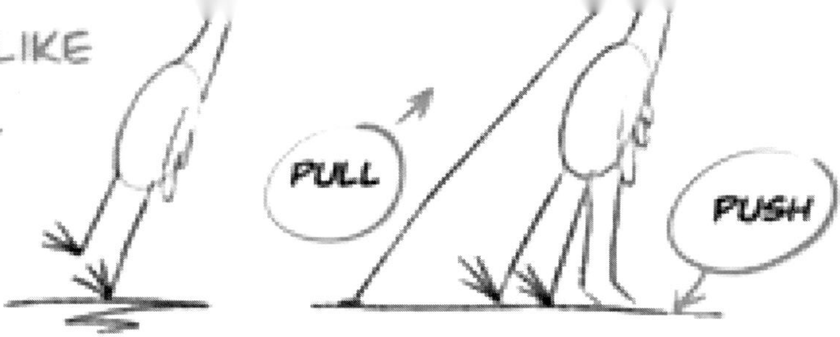

MAKE SURE TO GROUND YOUR BIRD.

Children of the Wartime Years

They still attended school, after the bombs fell,
   Scarching for, and hurriedly collecting, shrapnel.
"Coo, just the shape I want, says Jimmy, in a swap,
   As he juggles with a bagful of jagged old pieces,
And "You got a green marble for a reddun?" all a-hop,
   As, with excited fervour, surveyed his pals' releases.
        Then they all hurried on, must not be late,
      Their lessons to learn, in 1940, an heroic date!

But some were killed, already in their class,
   When Gerry decided to make his earlier vicious pass,
Little lives were lost forever, to the world outside,
   What might they all have achieved, had they lived on?
Some would soon be orphaned too, as parents died,
   How could they grow, unloved, their dear ones gone,
        Become sane, future British citizens, carefree,
      When, all around them, nations could not agree?

Fathers returning once, or twice, on home leave
   All too soon their young children would bereave,
Those loyal serving soldiers who would never again return,
   Leaving hard-pressed mothers struggling to make ends meet,
Poor little kiddies caught up in mayhem – bombs, maim, burn!
   Just rubble, gas fumes, spurting water, a flattened street.
        What had they done to deserve such hate,
      So much horrendous suffering, why this their fate?

Yet still the children who escaped, bounced back,
   Swapped comics, cards, naughtily climbed on rail-track,
Sang patriotic songs in school, ran races on Sports Day,
   Danced to 'Sir Roger de Coverley', scaled gym-frames in hall.
At assembly, all chanted hymns, learnt how to pray,
   Ran, skipped, played fast games, leap-frogged, threw a ball,
        They came bravely through, made for better times,
      Married, had children too, lived in happier climes.

And to their progeny had proud stories to tell,
That our Air Force turned the tide – London <u>never</u> fell,
Those same heroic children of the wartime, never bored,
now in their prime.

* * *

Little Orphans

Why are so many little ones born,
    Only to be rejected before the dawn
Of a first-drawn intake of breath,
    Unfed, unloved, to struggle unheeded, prior to death,
Discarded like an old worn-out coat?
    Oh, the ache that catches the throat.

They did not ask to enter the scene,
    These waifs, born in poverty in times so lean,
How can any mother throw her child away,
    Even tho' she has many others at the end of the day?
How can a father reject his own child,
    Leaving it prey to the elements wild?

Mother Teresa and her angels of mercy,
    Rescued hundreds from bins, often on hearsay,
In the heat and squalor and India's monsoons,
    Teaching poor women that babies are boons,
Not to be ill-treated when facing strife,
    She taught the world how precious is life.

The Dinner Party

When your guests arrive, right on time,
    And you are in a panic as your roux has curdled,
A once pristine apron seems covered in grime,
    Those unset dishes presenting yet another hurdle,
Sighing with relief as your beloved lends a hand,
    Promising to divert them away from the kitchen.
You knew he would be there, would understand,
    Yet to greet your friends you really are itching!
Oh why, oh why could they not have 'missed the bus',
    Then you'd not be in the midst of all this fuss?

As he greets them all and cheerily offers a drink,
    You can hear the laughter, at your expense,
And other guests arrive before you can blink,
    By now you feel so neglected and really tense
And all too ready to throw in the proverbial towel,
    As the vegetables have mysteriously cooked too soon,
So, by now, your mood has altered to one so foul.
    Oh, what the heck! You can't give them the moon,
When into your domain walks hubby, with sweet flowers
    And you try to forget you have slaved for hours!

Offering you a kiss and a welcome glass of sherry,
    He takes charge of the prawn cocktails and the wine,
Then it all ceases to matter, once you're pleasantly merry
    And the coq au vin portions are ready before time.
As you and your guests relax, they drink to your health,
    And soon you are serving the fresh fruit and cream.
It matters not that they all wish you great wealth,
    By now, you pray the magic will not fade, be a dream,
Your hard work has proved your dinner party success,
    And everyone's saying 'What a fabulous hostess!'

They depart, as you sink to your knees in the late dawn,
    Surveying clutter all around, the unwashed glassware,
Telling yourself it can all wait till the early morn,
    In a happy state, worn to a frazzle, you simply do not care!

The Trees of Moccas Park

Ancient, gnarled specimens survive here, generations old,
Wearing their summer gowns, after winter's cold,
Standing in stately grandeur, in haughty disarray,
Uncaring for the perfidies of nature thrown their way,
With a tremendous vitality emitted thro' Mother Earth,
Each tree, over all the years, has justified its girth.

Providing sheltered homes for all our feathered friends,
Tiny nooks and crevices, to the insect world they lend,
In the timeless 'Stag's Horn Oak', a rare beetle was found,
Oldest tree in the park, she proudly stands her ground,
Her long-dead branches, beyond her living crown extend
And the 'Moccas Beetle' moved on, other trees to befriend.

The 'Twin Peaks' tree, lightning-struck, shattered,
Regained its composure, although so badly battered,
Grew extra bark to heal the wound seared within its side,
Healthy young branches now grew strongly, it had not died!
For one trunk remained, flourished still, doing its best,
While a jackdaw family, in the dead wood, built a nest.

The 'Spanish Chestnut' came to our shores, in Armada days,
Known as 'Invader' has oval leaves, sharp teeth, to raze,
And produces Christmas chestnuts regularly every year,
With spiny shells, welcome provender for sheep and deer,
But the 'Horse Chestnut' with pretty flowers and sticky buds,
Has leathery, spiked fruits and conkers cascade down in floods.

And the 'Hollow Oak' may seem to be unstable in high breezes,
But is stronger in surging winds than many other trees,
Alive with grubs, from beetle-eggs, for woodpeckers, shy birds –
To burn her cast-off branches would have been so absurd!
Her rotten middle, stained red-brown by fungal red-rot,
Gives succour to birds, insects, tree-bats, in every hole and knot.

The 'Riven Oak' is a double-stemmed tree, hanging on to life.
Part of her fell into the pool where rotting wood is rife,
Just one branch remains, she is attached to life by a thread,
How long can it be, before this stalwart is finally dead?
Then the 'English Oaks' with acorns, cups, strewn on the ground,
Prevalent since the Ice Age, they will always be around.

The 'Knoll Oak', a champion tree, highest in the park,
Has great circumference like the 'Woolhope Oak', of
twisted bark,
Resembling the sweet chestnut, a strange trick nature played!
And then the 'Promontory Oak' with huge trunk, her
roots splayed,
Jutting over the pool, with willows and alders, still flouts her best,
Though one fine day, she will give in, sink down to her rest.

Altho' the fallen, smooth grey beech, pretty leaves can show,
With buds and flowers still fed, is hollow, by fungus laid low,
And the oldest ash has weird lumps and knobs, also eaten away,
For every felled tree, another will grow, God's purpose, to stay,
Encrusted with lichens, trees are shaped by circumstance,
To carry out a natural role, with grace, their stature enhance.

They stand tall and proud, short and stubby, well-endowed,
There is no finer thing to see, than the beauty of a tree.

Man's Survival

How can we, the world's people, the next millennium see,
    Unless we do intend, all wars to bring to an end?
And show ourselves more humbled, how concerned we can be,
    Become more sweet-natured, on each other to depend,
        Or else, however will humanity survive?
        It is for sure that it cannot possibly thrive.

When on earth will all the manifold killings ever cease?
    For nothing, this way, can be saved, seldom ever gained,
In happier things men and women ought to find release,
    Than to cause another's suffering, anguish and pain.
        We can all get along together, find better ways,
        To enjoy our fruitful, beauteous world, all our days.

We could bring about a paradise, an Eden of delight,
    Share in each others fortunes, helping in sorrow,
Why, oh why, must the evil in man, always spoil for a fight,
    When he could easily overcome adversity, find a new
                            tomorrow?
    Will that wonderful day ever dawn – not in _my_ lifetime,
    But can the good in man overcome? An upward climb!

The dire threat to the world, of global nuclear warfare,
    When innocents, like tiny babes, must inevitably suffer,
The fall-out, devastation, caused by catastrophic glare,
    And governments fail, find no solution, disputes tougher,
        What then can be said for peace in our time,
        When they cannot agree and fall into line?

The way ahead could very soon become more clear,
    If the powers that be supported one Council of Nations,
And could there be real strength, sustained, in all we hold dear,
    Making peace for the world a priority, bringing jubilations,
        For every country, every corner of God's earth,
        Could it be that man might, at last, show his worth?

We can only live in hope, put our trust in the One above,
That He will guide us, will not allow the races to pour scorn
Upon this wonderful planet He bequeathed us, with His love,
Where all our children's children will, some day, be born,
And will rule this earth with a greater wisdom,
So that, with real joy, His Kingdom, will surely come.

* * *

The Vagrant

He wanders idly, irresolute, lonely and forlorn,
Mayhap regretting the very day he was born,
A broken marriage, things he'd much rather forget,
This 'man of the road' is full of regret –
For he can never return, his children to see,
Ah well, they're better off without him, he'd agree.

He sleeps in barns, bus shelters, on a park bench,
Plastic bags for a pillow, your heart gives a wrench
That only his old overcoat will keep out the cold,
For, how can it do more, so threadbare and holed?
All that he owns kept in a small, rough sack,
Nothing of value – just the clothes on his back.

He'll beg others for food, any old thing will do,
Drinking from park fountains, he owns nothing new,
Hardly speaks to a soul, he's so sad and alone,
Just spare him a thought – as you hurry on home,
This forgotten human, put yourself in his place,
This vagrant – or tramp – has simply lost face.

The Village Church and Tavern

At day's end, the setting sun reddened the grey church walls,
  Catching mellowed brick, the rustic beauty of ancient
                                                    Manor Halls,
Such phenomena, from time immemorial, often has occurred,
  And has caught human breath, deepest inner senses stirred
Of homeward-going villagers, this sensuous vision to delight,
  Rejoicing at the hand of God, in such a primordial sight,
    They would linger awhile, glance heavenward, smile.

As they made their slow progress along a well-worn track,
  The phenomena had disappeared ere they had glanced back,
But then they would be halted, in their stride, yet again,
  When the clear eventide chimes made it very plain,
That night would soon descend, they <u>should</u> be home abed,
  From labours to rest, giving thanks for their daily bread,
    These villagers of old, returning to the fold.

Had they been to market, their goods to try and sell,
  Gathered kindling from nearby woods, fresh water from a well,
Their little ones to garner some ripened fruits to store,
  Against the cruel winter for those 'on the parish', the very poor?
The church their only saviour as they strove from day to day,
  As, in lowly state, they all came, to their Lord to pray,
    For sins to forgive, succour, guidance, to live.

Those ancient rural monuments, many a tale could tell,
  Summoning every kind of worshipper at the sound of
                                                    sweet bells,
From 'wattle and daub' cottages, the humbler folks abode,
  Dingy dens and draughty barns, in Sunday best they strode,
To the focus of their being, where its grey walls gave strength,
  The village church proclaimed its worth at every solid length,
    For Christian followers, contented or not, with their lot.

And soon, to drown sorrows, came the lowly drinking den,
Where mad demons often claimed the very souls of men,
The village tavern, for travellers, assumed the role of inn
And poor women had to rue the cost of terrible, wicked sin,
Comforting sobbing, hungry children, cruelly left in the lurch,
To whom could they turn but to kindly men of church?
To those whom God did intend, a listening ear to lend.

For men's pitiful wages could so soon be swallowed up,
And drunken fools lurched homewards 'in their cups',
Yet betwixt the two a fine balance could be reached,
As many a country parson to a sinful flock preached,
For all and sundry, in those times, to Sunday service went,
And always attendance from the Squire, or Manorial Gent.,
Keeping community spirit alive, the village to thrive.

And so, tavern and church both played their parts,
Grew old together and captured English hearts.

The Graveyard

Where stately stones their sad tales to the living recall,
    Almost obliterated by the savageries of weather, and time,
Lurching over, leaning drunkenly, where they might soon fall,
    Recounting little heart-wrenching verses, unhappily sublime,
        Telling of a tiny infant's untimely demise,
        Inscribed upon the heart, finds there no ease.

One glances at the precious grave, finding no comfort there,
    Just the grieving heartache, the terrible aching loss,
Words tell of sorrowing parental concern, appalling those
                                    who care,
    A memorial stone nature covers now, with lichen and moss,
        A little one who went up to heaven far too soon,
        Received with great love there, God's waiting-room.

We read, sadly, of young men in battle, who were lost,
    Of youthful mothers, taken by childbirth, illness, too early,
Whole families bravely struggling on, counting the cost,
    Leaving poor fathers to cope with the ensuing hurly-burly –
        Of life, unknowing to whom they might turn,
        To ease the pain, the dreadful loss – our eyes burn!

Around the graves, pretty meadow flowers thrive so well,
    Varied daisies, common mallow, poppies, sweet briar, self-heal,
Primroses, foxgloves, scarlet pimpernel, speedwell, time of
                                   year tell,
    Falling when the grass is mown, but, for now, their joy reveal,
        And, with the next blessing of refreshing rain,
        Spring back to life, parading their beauty again.

The sly old fox, the shy rabbit, prance upon hallowed ground,
    But will not be heard, by all resting in Heaven's sweet vale,
While the birds nest, roosting in nearby trees, they abound,
    Unheeding of the poignant tale each grave may detail,
        And share their space with the belfry bats,
        Who emerge at dusk, to pursue the gnats.

When the moon rides high in the sky, it is a haunted place,
  In the graveyard, where no willing soul ventures after dark,
Ghostly owls hoot and melancholy sets her awesome pace,
  And, in the distance, a dog will mournfully bark,
          Unheard, unseen, by all those here at rest,
          Yet once shared lives, drew breath, were blessed.

      Now safe in His loving care, they are blissfully unaware,
      And all is at peace, for life goes on, can never cease.

* * *

Lord, Swift to Save

When afflictions assault us, manifold,
Turn to the sweetest story ever told,
And Christ came down to earth, to save,
Recall how He died and rose from the grave,
He came to show us all the way, how to live,
    To pardon our enemies, how to forgive,
    To parley grievance with those who assail,
    Doing otherwise, His commandments we fail.

In all Christendom, His message is taught,
And we must obey, in this world upwrought,
    For He showed us the right way to behave,
    Pray for His guidance – Lord, swift to save.

Lifeboatmen

To exposed locations, thro' choppy, mountainous seas,
    With seamanship of an elect few second to none,
In all conditions and tolerating freezing icy breeze,
    Thro' storm-force winds they've rode the waves alone,
These brave men answer the call time and time again,
    Enduring stinging spray and lashing, tempestuous rain,
        Fetching home those they saved, from a watery grave.

In olden days, horse-drawn carriages were used,
    Pulling the craft of earlier times through the streets,
Over the hills, and thro' the towns, by impatient crews,
    Willing and ready to risk their own lives, in brave feats –
For those in peril on the sea, flound'ring in despair,
    The heroism and endurance of these lifeboatmen
                                    beyond compare,
        Volunteers to a man, saving lives their ultimate plan.

Struggling with their burden along a stony slipway,
    The men stumbling and righting their craft to launch her,
Must have needed great effort and enterprise in that day,
    And often all one family's men perished, went down together,
For the frames of their wooden boats could hardly withstand,
    The perilous, rampaging, monstrous seas, ferociously-fanned
        By storm-force gales, to make any heart quail!

Yet, unflinching, brave men have always answered the call,
    As the clanging siren's wail shrieked its message day or night,
And men of every age have rushed to their stations,
                                    whate'er befall,
    In all extremes of weather, the angry seas, they heroically fight,
Slipping the rescued into oilskins, warming, reviving with tots
                                    of rum,
    Men of the lifeboats have acted so, ever since Drake beat
                                    the drum!
        Smashing thro' high waves, none other than the brave.

Strong man-made materials are used to build present-day craft,
  And they slip effortlessly from strong moorings down

                                 the ramps,
Their crews still don oilskins in the same flying rush – keep abaft,
  As 'Skip' steers a stable up-to-the-minute lifeboat by

                               bright lamps,
Seagulls scream overhead, applauding great endeavours attained

                                   by all,
  Using communal effort, combined bravery, a wrecked ship

                          beyond recall!
  They saved many a one, returning, in triumph, a task well done.

And, as we lie safely in our beds,
These men of steel set forth again – and again,
To rescue those so filled with dread –
The debt we owe them, we must sustain.

The Church Congregation at Cliffe

They came, in all shapes and sizes, every age, one Sunday,
And I, a mere visitor, wondered at their fortitude and sheer pride,
In their very own beauteous church of God, midst an array
Of proud flags hanging high above our heads, closely allied
To their stout men and women at war, who gave and lost lives
Hailing from Cliffe, on the Cooling Marshes, in mem'ry survive.
        Here in Kent, where they still pay homage.

The bell-ringers pay out their merry 'come to church' tolls,
Reaching out over the plains, little villages and townships,
Plaintive, echoing peals awaken sleepy inhabitants, ringing calls
Reminding the worshipful, as they hastily come to grips
With their hurried household duties and myriad kitchen chores,
Prior to leaving homes, and a hasty departure, for the

                                    great outdoors.
        Another Sunday has come around and they <u>must</u> go!

They hasten over fields, or through the quiet streets,
So many diverse persons make their way to the call of bells
Whilst the lie-abeds linger on, repining, remaining discreet,
As they ring out sonorously, everywhere, to English vales

                                    and dells,
As they have rung out the good news in every century past,
And will continue to do so, their recipients to long outlast,
        Announcing, with joy, come worship the Lord!

Elderly matrons, upright pillars of both church and home,
With their unmarried daughters, and nieces of varying age

                                    and size,
And doddering old gentlemen lean heavily on canes, still come,
The semi-crippled arrive in wheelchairs, or on a frame relies,
Diligent worshippers hand out, one by one, hymn and

                                    prayer books,
To all and sundry who appear, then settle in favoured nooks,
        All of them, unashamed, to worship the Lord.

The young, the old and middle-aged, the very frail and the strong,
They greet each other joyfully, for there is nothing to fear,
All come together, to share, in heartfelt prayer and song,
This bond means another spirited Sunday morning is here,
All are led by their elected belief and love for our Lord,
They will all leave refreshed, renewed, prepared to raise

the sword,
Once again, invigorated, to face the world.

(And the bells ring out their glorious song,
Come to your church, happy believers,
For here you all belong.)

Departure

When grown children decide to 'fly the nest',
  You hope, and trust, that you've done your best,
As they set out along chosen paths of their own,
  And you realise your guidance they have long outgrown,
Yet they know you will be available, always there,
  Just the same, willing to support, you'll always care.

Altho' they have gone, you're just a 'phone call away,
  But you, and they, know you cannot live forever and a day,
Yet your words will still appear to them, in their minds,
  Altho' there will be temptations of so many varied kinds,
The love and trust you have given throughout the years
  Into their lives, will surely comfort them, constantly appear.

When they were little, and you were in sole charge,
  Life was simpler then, the horizon loomed large,
Imagining that the process of time dwelt on your side,
  Old age, with you, could never, ever have applied!
When holidays came around, children packed into the car
  As tidily as your luggage, as you set off for realms afar!

Your care for them, as little ones, knew no bounds,
  They all so loved the beach and happy seaside sounds,
And fond memories of sojourns into the English countryside,
  So often ending the day with a barbecue at the roadside,
On your terms then, they ran and played, came to you
                                              when called,
  And had they disobeyed, you soon showed you were appalled!

At each day's end, tired and elated, they all readily slept,
  Over each of their lives your vigil you fondly kept,
And now, time has long decreed, they have babes of their own,
  You are left wondering, 'Oh, where have the years flown?'
Ever aware that time is, at last, no longer on your side,
  But you have left them all a legacy and lovingly complied.

Family Ties

We never could imagine your leaving the ties that bind,
 Settling for pastures new, of a very different kind,
As you embark upon a vastly-strange new world,
 Into many new ways and customs soon to be hurled,
Altho' you have set your sights across those choppy seas,
 You are sure to feel many moments of great unease.

Step back in time and recall the little one you were,
 When, to your parents, loved ones, it never would occur,
That a lively, innocent, curly-haired small bundle of joy,
 Could one day sail across the ocean, with her boy,
Now, as you prepare to leave all that you hold dear,
 Will you let your mind travel back to bygone years?

To the time when family loyalties seemed to be as one,
 When teenage, and early married years, had barely begun,
And everyone seemed happy, content with their lives,
 Rearing youngsters, honouring marriage vows, loving wives,
Until outside influences proved to be far too strong,
 And one family member endured, alone, a great wrong.

She was no angel, I am sure she might readily agree,
 A victim of inner strivings, from womanly ills seldom free,
Yet dragged herself from this deep abyss, from a dismal life,
 Forgoing an unsafe marriage, becoming another man's wife,
She may always be unsure and needful of protection,
 Yet soon you will be gone, unable to help your defection.

Will you settle, try to be contented, find a new life to agree,
 Always putting on a brave face, an exile over the sea?
Or will your thoughts keep returning to the land of your birth?
 For, in truth, there is nowhere the same, anywhere on earth!
Yet, will you stubbornly remain and find some innermost peace,
 Or will your heart's real depths never find any release?

A Favourite Book

Hush, don't speak! This is one book you simply must complete,
Gone with the Wind or *Wuthering Heights* were both quite a feat,
But this volume *Restoration England* lore, holds you deep within
its spell,
One is soon transported back in time – to a fetid, living hell!
When thieves, rogues and pickpockets haunted every shadowy nook,
Their detailed activities well-contained within this history book,
When Royal intrigues and clandestine love affairs all played a part
And whole families, struck down by plague, were thrown onto a cart!

In shady London, 1665, leading up to the city's all-consuming fire,
When Charles II ruled, having everything he could desire,
At a time when his people starved, viciously fought and thieved,
And thro' the terrible curse called plague, hundreds soon bereaved,
The overcrowded prisons were simply filled beyond belief,
In the main, to feed young families, one became a clever thief!
The elite, as usual, entertained, and lived the luxurious life,
When poverty and sickness, amongst the masses, was absolutely rife.

Prince Rupert of the Rhine, a general, many a battle at his door,
Commanded the Royalist Cavalry, in the English Civil War,
Half-Stuart, he became a very noted and refined gentleman,
Who could have been a King of England, turning down the plan,
In loyal fealty to Charles and James, a most honourable Prince,
From Bohemia – he settled for an English life, in a London province,
Living at 'Awdes', also Spring Lane, he died from old wounds, giving
his all,
Lies interred in Westminster Abbey, as from grace he did not fall.

Many women of those times, humbled, made low by circumstance,
Abandoned, forsaken by others, turned to crime and had little chance
To better themselves, except thro' the elite decree, which enslaved them
And robbed them of their youth and pride, the vassals of old, old men!
Some to the theatre turned, protection finding there, food upon the table,
Others took in laundry or wet-nursed a wealthy woman's babe – if able,
And threadbare rooms were let for just 'one shilling and all found',
Where might disgraced, unhappy persons hide 'till better times abound'.

Transported to another sphere, deep in thought, in my armchair
                                                    snugly curled,
I dread a ringing telephone, or late caller, for I am lost to the world.
A clattering doorbell, when just absolute silence is what you need,
And you can hardly stir yourself, or bother, when the time comes
                                                    to feed!
Those dusting, hoovering and cleaning chores will simply have to wait,
And you act as though St. Peter is already at your gate!
But *The Vizard Mask* has proved so enthralling, a favoured tome,
One you simply cannot abandon – in the comfort of your own home.

At the Surgery

A busy receptionist says, "Take a seat, madam – or sir,
   Doctor's running a little behind schedule!" can often recur,
That he, or she, is really overstretched, no shadow of a doubt,
   But all you wish for, is to be seen quickly, then hurry on out!
To get on with your life, do your shopping, call at the Bank,
   Yet minus good health, not much is achieved, the Dr. thank,
     For his continuous, marvellous patience to all,
      From grace he cannot fall!

You sit and watch, marvelling at the unhurried pace
   Of life in the surgery, thinking 'Oh, why am I in this place?'
People all around sit quietly contemplating the floor,
   Or somewhere above each other's heads, or towards the door,
As yet more patients arrive to await their turn, jumping for joy,
   For they had just taken their place when the female 'tannoy',
     Announced, triumphantly, they are next to go,
     You whisper 'Please don't be slow!'

Patiently you sit there amid hustle and bustle – and agonise,
   Hoping that your fellows might kindly avert their eyes,
As your nervous tummy rumbles and groans irritably yet again,
   And you realise you have developed a sharp little pain!
It will not go away, so you quickly rise, daring to have a read,
   To fill your mind, fiddle with magazines, take no heed
    When the overhead message silently announces your turn,
    Oh, when will they all learn?

You are now wondering how much longer you can patient be,
   Why it all takes so long, you really cannot see,
And start to feel hard done by and shockingly overlooked,
   But, gradually, all ticks over well, they have not overbooked!
You need some understanding, now that you are really low,
   Then suddenly it dawns, your turn has come, things not so slow,
    And you rush to see your Doctor as tho' you are the late one,
    Rejoicing as he calls out, 'Do come!'

The Passion

Could I only have seen His agony
    I could not have felt more mortified,
More deeply wounded for Him who died,   *(Chorus)*
    So sorely troubled that I am so unworthy.

For I know how they mocked Him at Calvary,
    Of His poor mother's tears for her dear Son,
How they scourged and derided Him – for me,
    Then nailed Him to a cross, the wicked deed done,
And left Him to slowly die above that hill
    And I still see Him there as my eyes surely fill.

They made for Him a cruel crown of thorns,
    So piercèd, so bleeding was His brow,
Yet this world had rejoiced when He was born,
    How could they have scorned, rejected Him now?
As He died for our sins, our Lord and Saviour, vilified,
    Hung from that wooden cross, so cruelly crucified.

From my tear-filled eyes I now cannot see
    For I know how He gave His life for all,
To show the world of His love, to cleanse me,
    To save anguished sinners who, from grace, fall,
Son of the great Father in Heaven above,
    He showed me the way through His strong love.

(A hymn to be set to music)

He has Given Me Strength

In adversity, I need only to close my eyes, in silent prayer,
   That He might lift my spirit yet again, showing His care,
Knowing the weakness within me, and in the depths of gloom,
   It seemed I could be alone with Him, in a quite different room
In those self-seeking moments when He belonged to me,
                                                in quietude,
   For my self-pitying soul, I sought His wonderful magnitude,
                  And I am, once again, in control.

When I needed a reason to go on, trying to prove my worth,
   No one, but me, could truly have known, on this earth,
How depressing, how utterly self-destroying, others can be,
   Yet they may have had many personal troubles, the same as me,
For the weakness of my spirit, the many doubts in my ability,
   I reached the lowest depths imaginable – yet, in all humility,
                  He uplifted my soul and I am in control.

I sought His aid, when no other being their help could give,
   And prayed forgiveness for my sins, a better life to try and live,
I believe in His power and goodness, shall so do, all the days of
                                                my life,
   For He has upheld me, restored me, and banished my strife,
On Him I shall always lean for my support, omnipresent aid,
   Whenever I am anxious, terribly alone and very, very afraid,
                  Succour for my distressed soul; in control.

In quiet moments, He always imparts how much I mean to Him,
   He can uplift me, when all else seems so dark and dim,
Seek Him then, He will not fail you, but first seek your heart,
   When you find Him, in all His majesty, He will never let
                                                you depart,
Sublimely renewing your faith, once more, in your fellow man,
   Only obey His Commandments and believe in His
                                                wondrous plan,
                  And he will offer guidance – and self control.

   He has given me strength, and sent purpose into my life,
      I know He will not fail me, tho' there be further strife
                  And I am, once again, in control.

The Bluebell Wood
For all my Hawridge Friends
(8th/13th May 2003)

It was here, in this enchanted place, we paused awhile,
  Drowning in the surrounding beauty, the charm and guile
Of a myriad, softly moving, gloriously waving, bluebells,
  Breathing in the perfume-laden air of this fairy dell,
And I, transported back in time, to a childhood scene,
  Enraptured, as in this idyllic spot, countless blooms did glean,
    Yet now I would not harm their grace!

Catch them, while you can, in this merry month of May,
  They cannot stay, in glorious array, forever and a day,
Sweet perfection, blooming profusely at the very start,
  Their brightness will fade and must very soon depart,
But, for now, they proudly show their graceful heads, in unison,
  And, as we drink in their beauty, we pause to reason,
    That the hand of God is truly here.

We humbly bow, in adoration for this lowliest of flowers,
  Brought to fruition by the timing of April showers,
The colouring of bluebells remains their very own,
  There is no other shade to compare, no lovelier tone,
Graciously adorning green swards under cerulean skies,
  There is enchantment here; with bated breath and deep sighs,
    We linger, unwilling for the spell to break!

We drank in the sheer perfection of those English woods,
  At bluebell time, in delightful May; birds feed tiny broods,
Where the early cuckoo has called, upon his stealthy rounds,
  His merry call mingling with rustling woodland sounds,
And we have stayed, luxuriating, under a magic spell –
  Our companions to rejoin, reluctant to leave our dell,
    Yet anxious to impart our knowledge!

Where sweeps the graceful branches of many varied trees,
    The beech still reigns supreme, Queen of all the leas,
And, in this place, in all humility, we bow the knee,
    Remarking how closely it resembles a gently-rolling sea,
Doth our bluebell wood, this sunny day, in late spring,
    Which we have taken time to explore; our hearts sing,
        For we have found contentment here.

* * *

Victoria

Oh! Victoria, she has done it all again!
    The scarlet hussy has proved her worth
And brazenly defied the rigours of sun and rain,
    But when it all comes down to earth,
She really bears no secrets, this wonderful girl,
    For her children are so evident by the score,
Her excesses enough to make your hair curl!
    And you wonder, can she possible take any more?
This mother of all goodness – her plums so divine,
    At last she's ready now to drop her guard,
On her delectable offspring we can all dine
        And Victoria's reputation remains – unscarred!

The Lady with the Lamp – Florence Nightingale

Nursing was her endeavour, her aim, her principle goal in life,
This Englishwoman, from the New Forest, faced immense strife,
Beset by great official opposition, a pioneer of medical reform,
Leaving her family, the life she knew – she braved the storm,
To answer the call – from Harley Street – to the Crimean War of 1854,
She organised a nursing service, opening the world's door
For lesser men, lowly in rank, who called her 'Lady with the Lamp'.

The fight within her, against the odds, and prejudice so severe,
To relieve the British soldiers' suffering, she could only persevere,
And FN sailed, with 40 varied women, in late 1854, from Marseilles
To Constantinople, with 'The Times Fund', founded by Sir Robert Peel,
Backed by her own resources and Russell's report on the
$\qquad$ squalor endured,
She hoped to bring relief, and Sidney Herbert her position ensured,
As Secretary for War, in charge of sick and wounded, he opened
$\qquad$ the door.

Within a month, FN collated important facts, accruing information,
Sailing on a fast mailboat, 'Vectis', her small frame suffering violation
From sea-travel so terrible, so weakened, at Malta she remained aboard,
While her companions had freedom, and the little island explored.
Thence to Scutari Barracks Hospital, to their final destination,
No waggons for them, or their valued goods – such awesome desolation,
Everyone walked for more than a mile, tired, distraught, unable to smile.

Bare quarters awaited, no welcoming party, confined to limited space,
FN, in sole command, allotted wooden slats, decrepit chairs that
$\qquad$ night apiece,
On 5th November, icy cold, chilled, a kitchen found, made tea for
$\qquad$ the boarders,
And next day, sought a Dr. Menzies who, acting on prejudicial orders,
Made it plain that male orderlies only, worked in the wards, women to
$\qquad$ sew bags,
Roll and count bandages, menial tasks – yet wards were filthy, a stench
$\qquad$ to gag,
Men died from infections contracted here – so many departing – in
$\qquad$ abject fear.

The flower of the British Army, Guards and Grenadiers, sent to
                                        relieve Turks,
At The Bosphorus, doomed to perish; at beauteous Lake Devna,
                                        cholera lurked,
And Turkish Allies had to raise the siege of Silistria – their comrades
                                        had dysentery.
To be dumped by boat and mule into more misery, filth and despair
                                        at Scutari,
Already o'erflowing with cholera cases – no splints, chloroform,
                                        morphia, dressings,
Few doctors for thousands of brave men – Florence, despairing, the
                                        awful sessions
So set her back, wrote letters home and told of supplies cut to the bone.

At Sevastopol, sent to destroy the naval base, at the start,
Paltry Black Sea transport for 30,000 'kitted' men, all lost heart,
When tents, bedding, stores, medical supplies were left behind.
In Varna, Bulgaria – just 21 waggons for carting – so, maligned
British troops, victorious at Alma, with the French, had fought hard,
Paid the price, their wounded lay on manured straw, in a farmyard,
No litters or carts, at Calamita Bay; amputations by moonlight, end
                                        of day.

These sick, wounded men brought in ancient ships over the Black Sea,
Crammed with cholera cases, amputees flung around in such agony,
All wallowing in each other's ordure, in filthy clothing they lay,
No bedding, cups, buckets, tables, chairs, operational facilities that day,
As they poured into Scutari, praying for succour, from hateful disease,
Dysentery, scurvy, starvation, exposure to the elements, wintry unease,
The nurses proved their worth at last; straw bags filled, sore hands,
                                        so fast!

At Scutari, highly-efficient female nurses now showed their skills,
Idle for weeks, such waste, swallowing so many bitter pills!
As they converted bare, squalid buildings into a workable place,
But chaos reigned, fever and gangrene rife, terrible urgency apace,
As 'The Prince' went down, loaded with stores, in a frightful hurricane,
Now FN at last won official confidence – and made it quite plain
That monies, at her disposal, she _must_ spend, desperate men to defend.

Their amputated limbs, and numerous dead bodies, a sea-scum brought,
And, at Balaklava, this nightmare of utter garbage – contagion caught,
Though victorious at Inkerman, still Sevastopol did not yield and fall,
Then dreadful errors when supplies sent to Varna; men had given

their all

At the Crimean Front, as Florence knew well, when her actions at last
Brought them clean bedding and better food – her hands many clasped,
"We felt we were in heaven," they said, "in clean clothing, far

from dead!"

Against the odds, great prejudice and difficulties she overcame,
Converting bare, unclean, cold, damp barracks – led to her fame,
Into a workable hospital, her system adopted, used worldwide,
Rats and cockroaches her bane; officialdom, recalcitrance, swept aside,
Order achieved, washing, scrubbing, more attention to wounds and diet,
Her incessant vigilance won the day; she brought more peace and quiet,
Writing last letters for men's wives; held her hand, gave up lives.

How they had longed for a glimpse of her lamp, bobbing the while,
As she entered each ward to make her way past rank and file,
A little word here, a friendly smile there, soldiers in such dire pain,
She relieved suffering, eased journeys from this world, again and again,
A shred of comfort given when they were all so far from home,
Away from mothers, wives, children – yet still many to Scutari

had come,

And, in their turn, she assisted _them_, this angel of mercy, this gem.

Florence Nightingale, pioneer of the first movement for Red

Cross endeavour,

"Whose heroic efforts on behalf of suffering humanity",

forsaking never,

"Will be recognised and admired by all ages as long as the world

shall last",

Eulogiums for her noble life, nursing schools set up to honour her past,
The Order of Merit finally bestowed on a woman – but she

became blind,

Her iron frame enduring the cold and fevers of the Crimea, this

person refined,

Now suffered memory failure, not knowing the honours that hailed her.

She had driven herself constantly, gruelling labour, 40 hard years,
Yet lived on, deprived of memory, sight, sensation, not given to tears,
She could no longer read, could not speak in her final sad hours,
At noon, fading fast, the end came in August 1910; requesting
                                                          no flowers,
"No memorial whatever to mark the place where lies my mortal coil",
Bare markings on her grave at East Wellow, she was lain in soil,
Six British Army sergeants her coffin brought – and all distraught.

FN had been desperately ill at Scutari, with a fever so high,
And refusing rest, her resistance weakened, yet she put troubles by,
Recovering enough to carry on her good works as well as she might,
Uniting her nurses, who later revered her, for her upward fight,
'Gainst all the odds, returning quietly from the Crimea, life to resume,
Refusing interviews, all claims to fame, seeing stricken men at
                                                          their doom,
But she would never flaunt Crimean days – nor accept a grateful
                                                          nation's praise.

The Pond at Hitcham, in Spring

In the early, eerie light of a grey and sunless morn,
Viewing the scene, sombre and still, I kept silent watch,
Thro' the picture window, as the scene of a cold dawn
Unfolded before me, blue tits darting from their notch
In the deadened elm-wood of a gnarled old tree –
Sprawled at ludicrous angle o'er the pond by the lea.

Peacock, stretching his bright plumage, seemed to yawn,
To wonder if the time was right to venture from a lofty perch,
His companion, still sleeping soundly above, was not drawn
To descend, unless the warming sun might help his search
For tiny grubs, and juicy morsels, and leftover bread,
And pangs of hunger, to help his descent, from overhead.

Three drakes, victorious, had worn Duck to a frazzle,
And soon, tiny fluffs will skim hastily over their pond.
Keeping pace with mother, and she will prettily dazzle
Her suitors, with her graceful pirouettes; fawn charms so fond
For only one handsome male, who will be hers for life,
And the rejected ones, heads down, give in to Drake's new wife!

Upon this frosty morn, eerie screeches latterly fill the air,
As haughty peacocks stretch colourful wings in branches above,
And, condescending, fly down, in a whoosh! seeking their fare,
Now that the sun has risen and warmed them with his love,
They both spread their gorgeous feathers with whirring sounds,
And reward us all by displaying pretty colours all around!

A new, fresh awakening presents itself each morning,
As the rising sun appears, glistening on shimmering water,
Bright daffodils announce that Spring is here, edges adorning,
And a little black moorhen, laden with twigs, hastens to
                                                    court 'her',
She sits on a nest in tangled shrubs, and reigns supreme,
While he keeps busy, his offspring, as yet, just a dream!

A peaceful scene, broken only by Peacock's fearful squall,
Amid a flurry of quacks; now and then, Goose honks a reply,
Intensely white, protectively, she keeps guard over them all,
Gentle rabbits scurry hither and thither, tails a-bob, danger's nigh,
All kinds of sparrow call, tidying up tiny crumbs scattered soon
From delectable fragments of bread strewn in late afternoon!

Tree-creepers and wood-pigeons pay homage at the pond,
A busy robin guards his territory and Jenny Wren flits around,
Among the primroses, while flying ducks land – splash!
                                                from beyond.
Cause rippling rings to outward spread, then dive without
                                                a sound,
Another bright day has dawned, how lovely, how memorable
                                                the scene
Of utter tranquillity, a light breeze playing around
                                                meadows green.

And then, when Peacock, Duck, Drake, Moorhen, Goose and all,
Once again retiring for their rest, to bush, nest and tree,
The flame of the sun is gradually sinking, its reddened ball
Casting a pinkish glow over the calm water – I bow the knee,
For the contentment this therapeutic little backwater brought,
As little things rustle, I thank God – for the message He taught.

Injustice

How can it happen, time and time again, such hate
   For fellow men, that all reasoning flies out the door?
When, cringing in stone cellars, praying the onslaught to abate,
   A sobbing, fearful race, whether they are rich or poor,
Have to endure such terror from oppressors, night after night,
   When bombs rain down on the innocent, cry for their plight.

Wreaking a terrible vengeance for past misdeeds – is so wrong,
   For the frightful suffering visited upon these innocents,
Who are made to pay for political errors of judgement, and long
   For the perpetrators of evil to go away, they are incensed
That, despite world opinion, the bombers inhumanely kill,
   A nation's children – abandoned – this cannot be God's will?

So much injustice in our world, as tiny babies without sin, die,
   They should not be exposed to terror – starvation – desolation,
And sorrowing parents cannot protect them, can only sigh,
   As the hateful maladjustment of principles brings isolation
From the way of life they hold dear, to which they pray for return,
   But they can only watch and grieve, to see their cities burn.

Nations of the world united, in sympathy for their plight,
   Yet still the mightiest followed through their conquering plan,
And paid no heed to lesser men, who may have won the fight,
   If only given more time to try and save the day; they began
With energy and such high hopes and progress steadily made,
   But, in the end, history will prove they really were betrayed!

Brought down by the greed of humankind,
   Men, and women, of the Arab-world suffer and cry,
For their countries and culture – their sick and blind,
   A new way thrust upon them, they can only defy,
As their conquerors reel from revulsion so strong
   Of a downtrodden people, so wickedly wronged!

Meanwhile, a nation suffers, little children burned and maimed,
    And the men who perpetrate such injustice, living in fine style,
Should themselves be cast into Hell's fiery furnace, and blamed,
    Damned forevermore by a Higher Council, for egotistic guile,
Greed and immorality and sheer hypocrisy in their wicked plan,
    It seems that these false, stupid men will never bend,
But God, sitting in judgmental array, needs the will of man,
    For He sees so much injustice daily – when will it ever end?
        Unceasingly, thousands of lives are daily lost,
        Unjustified, the terms in human cost.

This Fair Land of Ours – England

She is deeply-steeped in the annals of time,
Men and women have fought, and died, for her prime,
Each blade of grass and age-old leafy trees,
Every nook, cranny, and lively, whisp'ring breeze,
The birds on the wing all tell of her great past,
The pride of her people, who have held on fast
                To her greatness – this England.

Her verdant pastures and secret hiding places,
Our timeless ancestry derived from numerous races,
This achingly pleasant land of our forebears,
You mock her at your peril – no one dares!
Her timelessness outweighs the weakness of reason,
And many defiant ones have died for proven treason –
                A proud past will not tolerate. This England.

Her forests of old, well-trodden by countless feet,
The valleys and woodlands of this ancient seat,
Every castle moat, and walls, and outlying farmstead,
And medieval Courthouse, wherever the English had tread,
Every shadowy corner of a field, for meetings clandestine,
Where rustic hedgerows withstand the test of time,
                Their secrets well-hidden, for England.

Lords of the manor ruled fast, in their day,
While serfs tilled the soil and brought in the hay,
Fields divided, remain intact, hedges set and placed,
Villeins, bound by feudal service to liege lords, all embraced
The same laws of Henry II, dispensed by 'Justices in Eyre',
And equally enforced to both rich and poor, to be fair,
                No person above the law – in England.

The splendour of our cathedrals and cloisters so fine,
Evoke our gratitude to medieval builders of that time,
When Saxon and Norman masons, carpenters and glaziers,
Remained on site, completing their work, kept warm by braziers,
These Englishmen, proud of their skills, worthy of deep pride,
Where spires of hope speak of God Eternal, for whom men died,
                For His glory – in England.

The Royal rise of Egbert's Saxon line, still remains,
King Alfred, his grandson, built sturdy ships and defeated Danes,
Great names of note, and everlasting fame, as handed down,
Tell of numerous battles and conquerors of English renown,
Leaving a legacy of tell-tale place names to stay forevermore,
In these isles of a United Kingdom our ancestors fought for,
                And still guarded today – for England.

Our Morris dancers may not in winter perform, they would
                                                freeze!
In national dance, sing all kinds of ditties, as English as oak trees,
All have more than one attire to ring the changes, to little
                                                tinkling bells,
We take immense pride in them, and all our serving,
                                                marching fellows,
And in these islands of mystical delights, the variety of scene
                                                a surprise,
Our adherence to fair principles in a land of opportunity
                                                and enterprise,
                Ladies and gentlemen – a toast, to England!

Where whispers every blade of corn, grafted, for generations,
And highwaymen haunted English lanes 'gainst the pattern of
                                                our nation,
Each great, or lesser creature, lain to rest, in this precious earth,
The patriotic singing at the renowned Albert Hall, all prove
                                                our worth,
Our pride in our flag of St, George, billowing from
                                                buttresses high,
In our dear land, for whom exiles long to return, so they can die
                And still their longing – only for, this England.

The Parting

Standing alone, at your graveside,
Feeling dejected and so blue,
I pondered on why you had left me,
And why did it have to be you?
But everyone said, it's God's purpose,
He'll tap your shoulder and say 'Come home,
I need you to tend Eden's sweetest flowers,
And never again need you roam,
       Your place is here, in Paradise,
       On your life there was no price.'

As I laid my blooms upon your grave,
And spoke my thoughts to your dear heart,
I wondered anew why you had gone ahead,
Why God had decreed that we should part,
When there was so much more we had to do,
So many places to go, so much yet to see,
But He wisely knew that the time had come,
That first it should be you, and not me,
       To find your loved ones up above
       And tell them of our infinite love.

So while I await my turn to join you,
And hope you may hear my voice, as I pray,
I shall comfort our children and tell them,
I know that I shall find you one day,
Just be patient, my love, I will join you,
When God decrees I have done my best,
To lessen the heartache down here below,
For He alone knows I'll be put to the test,
       Just keep my love within your heart,
       Then never again will we two part.

Motherhood

Watching a child swinging her doll, crooning sweetly,
Chastising, then soothing and loving it so completely,
This, then, means motherhood and, in a little one's heart –
Rapture, but one fine day, she'll awaken, when childhood departs,
      To find the nest flown and she will be alone.

If motherhood means letting them go, you know not where,
Yet still you have to show that you will always care,
That an ever-open door will give sanctuary to the lost,
Where wounded spirits recover, you will not count the cost,
      For this child of yours, now safely at your door.

Motherhood means great sacrifice and so much giving,
So much lassitude and forbearance, constantly living
In the hope that, one day, peace from your solace is found,
When that wounded child finds strength to turn her life around,
      Because you were there, giving your care.

When you recall your simple joy at each wondrous birth,
And never a child to equal yours anywhere on earth,
Your firstborn a special moment as it's never come before,
Tears bedim your eyes at the memory, for she had opened a door
      And found a niche in your heart, never to depart.

Then, another happy event, the long-awaited robust boy,
And your third surprise, a tiny girl with fine curls, bringing joy,
Followed by a fourth welcome child, your second fine son,
To complete a happy family when he decided to come,
      Many years between, then he arrived on the scene!

Motherhood is unashamed, unstinting, not seeking reward,
Epitomised, the instant you gaze on a new-born babe, adored,
Crying piteously, helplessly relying on a mother's loving care,
Forever constant, in agony of mind, calming, soothing, you
                                  are there
      To nurture a troubled little soul, your lifelong goal.

Kilvertian Remembrances

This literary genius, devout Christian, man of his time,
Diarist and talented writer of poetry, deep and sublime,
Penning thoughts on the beauty of his beloved Welsh hills,
This tall, darkly-handsome young man, remembered still,
      Setting out his life, in answer to God's call,
      For the wellbeing of others, he gave his all.

A strong walker, loving and communing with nature so well,
His ministrations, with sincerity given, at many a funeral knell,
Meant so much to his Welsh flock, growing to love this able man,
Who so quickly engrained himself in the everyday plan,
      Becoming a part of their lives, both rich and poor,
      A welcome visitor at very many an open door.

Francis Kilvert, Reverend gentleman, mentor and friend,
The diverse souls he met and soon knew well, could depend
On his charitable nature, giving to all his ministering care,
A socially able person, mingling freely with others, and aware
      That here, in Clyro, lay his true vocation,
      To preach our Lord's word, in this location.

A life which differed greatly to a curate's humbler role,
Was offered to this fine man, whose innermost soul
Had settled for the rural Wiltshire scene of his youth
And had not envisaged a harsher living, in very truth,
      Nor to leave so soon his loving family life,
      Kilvert knew what it meant to feel strife.

A man who wrote compellingly, with such moving force
That parts of his diaries could engender our self-remorse,
To read his works meant deep awareness of so much beauty,
To the very depth of his being and descriptive of his duty,
      For his parishioners, both young and old,
      Whom Kilvert embraced within his fold.

In the Welsh hills he settled down, a harder role defined,
An often lonely man, yet thankfully, very sound of mind,
Delighting in the 'distant azure mountains', portrayed in
                                              his lines,
Then, not so alone, when in fine or humble company he dined,
          Carrying out the work of the Lord, in his prime,
          Sorrowfully leaving this world, well before his time.

* * *

Blindness

We cannot know, the ones who clearly see,
  Of the blind man's affliction, his dread of life,
Unless, without sight, we may become like he,
  With faltering steps, relying, heavily-leaning,
                              in our strife,
Depending on other's sympathy, hoped-for goodwill,
  Knowing how hard it becomes, to climb that hill.

We cannot know his innermost turmoil and pain,
  Of his dark world, his many doubts and fears,
When he can no longer see beauteous earth again,
  And depression comes too readily, reducing him
                              to anxious tears,
But the kindness of our words, instant helping hands,
  Will convey real sincerity – that he understands.

A Child's Trust

From the moment she takes her first uncertain steps,
To the heart-pulling time when she has to move on,
This tiny scrap, nestling in your arms, has assuredly crept
Into your mind, your soul, since the day she was born,
Becoming right then the very reason for your living,
Demanding your love and the whole of your giving,
   Now that she's here, in your care.

From the time he arrived, her little twin knew,
You would fight for his existence, his right to live,
Together they will sense they can so depend on you,
That all their misdemeanours you'll readily forgive
As you guide, and guard them, along the stony path of life,
Never to betray their trust, shielding them from strife,
   In an uncertain world, in your care.

From babyhood to tottering infant, and far beyond,
These little ones rely so much on your loving support,
From the minute they entered the scene, wailing and blond,
To draw their first breath, your devotion deeply caught,
So vulnerable were they, so innocuous and sweet,
Portraying enough guile and innocence, never to deplete
   That bond of love and care.

From the day they were born, relying on you alone,
Those small trusting hands in yours, quelling tears to fall,
And then the sweetest of smiles to melt any heart of stone,
Saving the day yet again with patience beyond the call,
For a child can bring so much joy, and so much fun
Into mundane lives; so much pride, laughter and warm sun,
   We cannot betray their trust, in our care.

"Suffer the little children to come unto me", Jesus said,
Little souls so dependent on us, for love and daily care,
Radiating peace when, in repose, we gaze on sleepyheads,
And wonder how anyone could harm them, lying there,
Then cherish, honour and guard them well and, in their turn,
They will, in the future, repay with love, little ones who learn.
　　　Who will be in *their* loving care.

* * *

Guiding Days

I made my promise, answered the call
And, willingly, tried to give my all,
For the Guiding movement so fine,
Helping young girls to 'toe the line',
To think of others by 'lending a hand',
To serve God and Queen, love their land,
Respect their elders, give sibling-care,
Taking no more than their fair share.

Oh, how I loved those guiding days,
Tho' errors made, far from right always!
I would not have missed the fun and games,
Recalling, with ease, those Brownie names!

(With love from 'Brown Owl' – or 'Robin'.)

The Joy in Musical Release

Entranced, I heard a maestro playing a violin in tune,
    In a coastal town, on a fine and sunny afternoon,
Each cadence of melodic sound brought such sweet refrains
    Across the gentle, balmy sea air, their haunting strains
Encompassed my thoughts with peace; troubles found release.

Then, transported with delight, operatic arias fill the air,
    Carrying me spiritually to a far-off land, and I have no care
As the lilting voices blend, so perfectly, in splendid song,
    They have the power to lift my soul high, carry me along
On a wave of pure, unfettered joy; my pleasure cannot cloy.

Talented musicians who reward us, with melodious sound,
    Deserving of our gratitude, their copious scores abound
With nostalgic, lingering tunes that may the heart beguile,
    Such depth of meaning conveyed in pure, harmonious style,
So well-serenaded that joyful day; worries faded away.

And toward evening, the sound of tinkling piano keys,
    Carried on the still, heady night air, designed to please
Each passer-by; such clarity in the resonant notes,
    Each sweet melody played drifted out to sea, to float
Upon the dancing waves; peace of mind to save!

Then I am mindful of the balm that filled my soul
    At Verona, for the operas; divas and tenors played their role
To bring us well-loved airs, all voices so perfectly blended,
    As prima donna sang with baritone and bass, her
                                voice ascended
To the heavens above; operatic arias telling of love.

In concert, cantatas and oratorios, in heavenly voice,
    The world over, divine music sung, and hearts rejoice,
Yet also, pleasing strumming on a guitar, Spanish style,
    And accordions, played romantically, in French cafés, awhile,
To bring sweetness and delight; upon a balmy night.

And native to our islands, the Welsh harp finely strung,
    The jolly Irish fiddle, Scottish pipes and drum,
English lutes, and lyres, viols and spinets, of early Tudor time,
    And famed orchestras to convey composers' work sublime,
On reflection I pause; all are so worthy of our applause.

* * *

'The Stables' Museum

This little place so set the pace,
A real challenge to those who cared,
For Chesham folk it has earnt a place
In this historic, ancient town – and we dared,
A team of devoted volunteers all-a-steady,
Accepted the challenge and answered the call,
When 'The Stables' was offered, all proved ready
For hard slog, real effort, but many a brick wall!
Yet we never gave in - now 24 years later,
Our town, of Saxon origin, a museum can boast,
For the general public we really can cater –
And might there be a resident ghost?

The Hunt

Panting for breath, heart thumping, she took flight again,
Distantly she heard the anxious baying of the hounds,
This poor, fleeing, terrified creature, could not restrain
Her exhaustion, as she fled, in leaps and bounds,
      Heading for some dense woodland cover, to hide,
      Seeking sanctuary to recover some pride.

Her rib-cage heaving, and shaking from her fear,
The ruddy fur wet with sweat, to her flanks,
Eyes staring, waiting patiently for them all to appear,
The vixen knew the end had come, cowering under a bank,
      This lone, exhausted being, could only await
      The loud cries of tormentors – and her fate.

She would never again hear her mate's shrill bark,
The wily dog-fox silhouetted 'gainst a moonlit sky,
As he called to her to seek him , in the covering dark,
Stealthy creatures of the night, cubs hidden nearby.
      All would be lost, the quiet life they had known,
      For soon, the little vixen would be torn to the bone.

Her cubs may then cruelly starve to death, or abused
As objects to be torn apart by 'learning' young hounds,
Had they come into this shameless world, accused
As only vermin, these pitiful babes? On what grounds?
      Can they justify these rampant slaughters,
      Which can only appeal to certain disporters?

Could she help her instincts, how God had made her,
This silent, cunning, amber creature of the night,
Her approach unheard until final moments occur
Putting all other small prey in her path, to flight?
      But she had to live too, as He decreed,
      To replenish her larder, little ones to feed.

A little rested, panting still, she awaits the end,
Straining her ears for hounds – _could_ the scent be lost?
No distant barks, she might break cover and homeward wend
Could she live, breathe another day, and not be tossed
      To the pursuant, eager, baying hounds?
      Hush, step quietly please, not a sound,
      And she – goes free.

The Beauty of East Anglia

Through th'undulating, golden fields of corn,
Freshly stacked and glowing bright in the sun,
Amid the rolling acreage, we wandered, reborn,
Elated, in these ancient farmlands, contented among
    The folks, whose lineage came from every sphere,
    Overseas conquerors, who proudly settled here.

In that magic glow of an East Anglian sky,
Distant church spires, so visible, in a flat landscape,
The brash, raucous cries of geese, as they southward fly,
Haunting our reverie, in V-formations they drape
    Across the ageless migratory course of old,
    Returning to fresh pastures, back to the fold.

From Kings Lynn, round the coast, to Caister-on-Sea,
Then Southwold to Aldeburgh, Felixstowe to Southend,
The discovery of these coastal regions, seen from every quay,
Brings the beauty of Britain to the fore, you can depend,
    This marvellous coastline, stretching for miles,
    In all its glory and we lingered the while.

In gathering rainclouds, or under glowing golden skies,
The lure of Constable country, where 'The Haywain' he'd paint,
And Willy Lott's cottage still remains, where rooks' cries,
In the tall trees, by the River Stour, and villages so quaint,
    Led us to East Bergholt church and spire so high,
    So essentially English 'gainst the deepening sky.

Hastening on to find the confluence of the Stour and Orwell,
Supping at "The Butt and Oyster", water-lapped edge of Pin Mill,
To Shotley Gate's hazardous ride to busy boatyards, pell-mell!
Then to Erwarton's church where Anne Boleyn's heart is still,
    At rest, in its casket, and her presence remains,
    Mother of Elizabeth, Henry's memory stains!

The broad sweep of the land, Tudor dwellings, ancient mills,
Fascinating names, Monks Eleigh, Stoke-by-Nayland,
Nedging Tye,
Gusting breezes over Rattlesden Airfield, sensing Yankee
ghosts still
Haunt the runways where giant 'birds' once used to fly,
    Scattering the starlings, on sun-glinted wings,
    While timeless nostalgic memories, linger and cling.

Have No Regrets
(For Tommy)

As little children, we seldom have any cares
And follow that certain path, with gradual ease,
To maturity, trustful and hoping, in our fervent prayers,
For guidance, that ourselves, and others, we shall please,
    And soon find that time does not stand still,
    Leaving you stranded, so many dreams to fulfil.

If you wait around for a more favourable day,
You are sure to find that it may never come,
Time waits for no man – you must not delay,
In wasting precious chances, your state of mind numb.
    You thought, when you were small,
    Old age would never come and call!

There's so much to do before you're 'over the hill',
High hopes flew, as time passed swiftly by,
So much left undone, too much to achieve still,
All the many challenges of life will speedily fly,
    So gather those rosebuds while you may
    For they will be gone the very next day!

Don't be an idler, bedbound and lazy,
Get on and do all that your heart is set upon,
Before your active thoughts become somewhat hazy,
And Old Father Time defeats you, your youth gone,
    No good your seeking a soft landing,
    When rampaging time has left you standing.

So make hay while the sun still shines,
And try to remember this ancient adage
When, one day it dawns, and you have worry-lines,
'Time and tide wait for no man', turn the next life-page,
    Achieve cherished goals in the glowing sun,
    Before your time on earth is ever done.

All too soon, winter bleakness creeps on us unawares
And you will soon know that those aching limbs
Are much too weakened to climb those tedious stairs,
Long, long ago, before the tired memory could dim,
      When you reached the heady age of reasoning,
      Following your star, prior to the dreaded seasoning!

* * *

Live for Today
(For Michael and Sharon)

It is futile to remain in the past,
      For nothing on earth can you gain –
Altho' so many events left you aghast,
      They cannot be altered and only bring pain,
So shelve those sinister thoughts and fears,
      For endless bad memories only cause tears.

It is incredibly hard to forgive and forget,
      Those persons who have cause you such wrong,
Yet they must know they are in your debt,
      Their conscience haunting them all life long,
So live for today and ignore the sad jeers,
      You <u>can</u> outlive them – through your happiest years.

Market Day

Oh, the joy! the sights and sounds and the smell,
As the vendors cry their wares, forever trying to sell,
Amid the hustle and bustle and total confusion,
Another busy day for them, laden stalls in gay suffusion,
Offering saleable goods to all and sundry and unwary,
On this day of all days, the sellers' craft will never vary,
   And market day is round again!

To sense the liveliness and well-being of all,
And to savour the atmosphere, outlying villagers call,
At this happiest of meeting places, where old friends meet,
Opinions exchanged right there, in the bustling street,
Rampant high spirits survive, mid challenges galore.
There are freshly-baked loaves, and cakes by the score,
   Another frantic market day has arrived.

Small boys weave in and out of absolute chaos and din,
Mothers comfort or scold the wailing infants they all bring,
And your nostrils lead you on to a stinking fish-stall,
Eagerly sought and bargained for, at the monger's call,
By the humble poor haggling over the unfair prices,
While rich merchants wander off, amused, to other devices,
   But all are welcome, on market day!

Farmers bring their gobbling turkeys and bleating lambs,
Penned with ducks, hens and suckling pigs, missing their dams,
Produce of the smallholding too, the groaning vegetable stands,
Eggs piled high in baskets, wives prod fruit, money
          changes hands,
Caged birds sing, and sales flourish in this topsy-turvy scene,
Of medieval salesmanship at higgledy-piggledy village green,
   Nothing much has changed, on market day!

Laughter

Life takes on a whole new dimension,
When laughter rings out as clear as day
Nothing else compares, for easing tension,
Releasing the spirit, as though a roundelay,
A carousel of light-hearted good humour,
Caught on as quickly as though a rumour!

Laughter can be such infectious fun,
It can ease your many troubles away,
Over adversity, victory can easily be won,
Those problems will keep for another day,
How much better not to wear a frown,
For that will only keep you down!

Look at the funny side of life, whenever you can,
Make living worthwhile, have a good smile,
Fall about with laughter, to be a happier man,
Bring the ladies some cheer and use your guile,
Keeping 'your sunny side up', those oldies all knew,
Eased wartime blues for many a long queue!

For those sad moments life caught you unawares,
Convince yourself that laughter will return,
Remember that someone, somewhere, really cares,
And life's hard knocks we all need to learn,
It's not easy, sometimes, to force a laugh,
Yet doing so could set you on a happier path.

Having a good laugh at your own expense,
Can keep your sanity – and the Doctor away,
If you're bubbling with mirth, it just makes sense,
You can, once again, bring sunshine to your day,
Keep 'rolling in the aisles', have a real chuckle,
Bright and clear as a bell – just loosen that buckle!

God is Weeping

When little children are needlessly slain,
    Causing our Lord such immense pain,
Wreaked on earth thro' man's intense greed,
    Bringing hatred, and wars, that fester and breed,
How can you imagine that He is sleeping,
    When, for the world He came to save, God is weeping?

He is distraught, and weeps, when religious persecution
    Rears its ugly head, for it is never the solution,
To the manifold sickness throughout the world,
    Bred in man's psyche, in God's name, then hurled
Throughout the many lands of His Kingdom,
    God is weeping – can our endurance overcome?

For the racial intolerance endemic everywhere
    Still seething and bubbling, this Hitlerite flare,
Smouldering on, with its demonic destruction,
    And no reasoning at all in any man's deduction,
For when God decreed we were all equal,
    He is weeping so, for the ghastly sequel.

For the hatred fostered in the hearts of men
    And consistent renewal of prejudicial phlegm,
Constant torture and imprisonment, deprivations,
    For coldness and hunger, thirsty, famished nations,
Imagine then, those heavy, torrential downpours
    Are truly God's tears for the breaking of His laws.

For man's iniquities, He shouldered the blame,
    He suffered agonies on the cross of shame,
When man decreed His goodness on earth should end
    He had come to redeem us all and did not portend,
That mankind, so base, might ever sink so low,
    Lost in Satanic power; God's tears overflow.

The Fortunes of the Song-Group

Once again, unto the fray, my dear old friends,
And all aware of the applause ringing in our ears,
For upon each other our true success depends.
Whether our singing means laughter, or brings tears
    We doggedly pursue until the very end,
    Every note and cadence as voices blend.

The pleasantries of song, when sung in unison,
And then we are aware of every little nuance,
As we take up our positions and issue forth, in throng,
With such pleasing sound, we adopt a defiant stance,
    But false notes can set the nerves ajar
    And, struggling for equilibrium, present no bar!

For disharmony brings anxiety, a lovely song marring,
But we are only amateurs, trying hard to please,
And pray that our audience will not be set a-jarring,
As we straighten any sour notes and put them all at ease,
    Ad-libbing whenever words go astray,
    Never giving in and ready for the fray!

Flustered arrival, all are aware, upsets the balance,
And we all need the written word, feeling no shame,
For we all know we have sufficient talents,
To bring sweet harmony to our choruses, and claim,
    That the clarity of a varied mixed voice,
    Is enough to make any audience rejoice!

Umpteen kind words encourage us to call again
For we can still delight many dear old people,
With our noted pianists to accompany each refrain,
They all acclaim our worth as high as a steeple,
    We are not pros – aha! ahem! but reach high notes,
    Trilling sweetly as songbirds, spirits afloat!

An Ever-Changing Lake

When he arrived, the lapping water serene,
A tiny breeze causing wavelets to ripple and flow,
He could only marvel at the wonderful scene,
Spread invitingly before him; his heart aglow,
As he cast his line in hopeful anticipation,
His spirit soared heavenward, with elation.

Then the sunshine, which had begun the day,
Rapidly changed his view of the tranquil lake,
Never had he seen such dramatic change, as it ebbed away,
Replaced by blustery skies, a storm about to break,
Like a cauldron boiling up the water that day,
Came a ferocious downpour, and his feet turned to clay!

A change in fortune had crept up unawares,
And the once placid lake became a vale of tears,
As the sad, but ardent, fisherman now angrily glares,
Grieving the loss of another fine trout, he fears,
The pouring rain soon drenched him to the skin,
The sky black as the Ace of Spades, he gave in!

The icy coldness of a late wintry afternoon
Had chilled his bones and broken his resolve,
Glancing at the turbulent waters, he prayed that soon
The burgeoning raindrops would no longer revolve
Around his little domain, there on the muddy bank,
Yet came another huge downpour, and his heart sank!

He longed for the warmth and comfort of home,
As he desolately packed away all his sodden gear,
Watching the wildfowl huddled on their island, alone,
He envied their companionship and longed for a beer,
Then the storm drained away, the winds eased, came balm,
As the rainclouds passed over, his soul found calm.

A Dungeon Prison
(For Prisoners Everywhere)

A hearty man, and able, in his youth,
Led away into darkness, for speaking a truth,
To spend his days, in a futile waste,
His nearest and dearest he finally embraced,
No amount of pleading, his captors could shake,
To shirk their parlous duties, too much at stake,
    And so, the poor wretch, this chastened day,
    His deepest fears they would not allay.

On leaden legs, they hauled him away,
Dragging and shoving him along, on feet of clay,
Into the castle dungeon, hideously thrown,
To spend his days and nights, lost and alone,
In darkness, suffering the affliction in his soul,
Only squealing rats for company, in this hell-hole,
    They had their freedom, could come and go,
    He had only fragile hope, in the midst of his woe.

No early release for him, how the time lagged,
When, from that last embrace, he was dragged,
His own kin left to agonise, to ponder on his fate,
Shaking with fear, then through the castle gate,
For supporting a system, sadly his Lords did not agree,
And so the only answer must be, his early captivity,
    In vain, on deaf ears, he pleaded for his life,
    That he would not leave sorrowing children and wife.

They chained him to a hard, damp wall,
Shivering and cold, at first he'd loudly call,
But his rough, abusive gaolers fed him only once a day,
Unable to exercise, his aching limbs gave way,
He soon became a gibbering, mental wreck of despair,
Doomed to grow old before his time, in his stinking lair,
    His anguish and torment of mind, left to go rotten,
    This able young man, liberty gone, soon forgotten.

Migratory Birds

Rudely awakened from my deep slumbers,
   In the translucent light of early morning,
I heard the strident calls, in varying numbers,
   Of Canada geese, departing, the daylight dawning,
Honking their noisy way to warmer climes
   To settle in old nesting-grounds and seek fresh grain,
In V-formations, clamorous, fine birds in their prime,
   Their loud calls echo, in Autumn skies, again and again.

The swallows, and their kind, long since gone
   I had observed from my high window, in the sky,
What awful buffeting winds will carry them along,
   Awaiting their flight, many to survive, yet some to die?
Still their cavortings and graceful antics remain,
   And will long stay alive, to keep in memory sublime,
As they flew, so bold on the wing, a height to attain,
   In that moody October sky, heading for fairer times.

Wheeling and curving thro' Autumnal skies,
   The early sun casting a wondrous pink glow, on pretty wings,
Scudding rain-clouds urge lone stragglers to fly,
   And soon they will all be gone, bright flocks of starlings,
For they stayed far too long, these late migrations,
   And we shall have to await their cheerful return,
But others will come again, in numerous variations,
   Announcing their presence – for sweet Spring we yearn.

Late Autumn Delights

The chestnut trees are so entrancing,
    In shades of russet-gold hues,
Stirring winds bring their leaves a-prancing,
    And soon they'll know old wintry blues,
But 'though we witness yearly change,
    Still yet Old Nature will rearrange,
        In manifold goodness.

How colour-strewn are the fields,
    Now that farmer's tasks are done,
In early Autumn giving up rich yields,
    Ripened and matured by late summer sun,
And we, the fortunates, will be daily fed,
    And nurtured by our Supreme Head,
        Who decrees all.

And we can live and hope anew,
    For Spring, that life-giver, to call again,
Who, though keen Autumn winds all blew,
    And slender little birches shed golden rain,
Meant England's fields will shine once more,
    To fill our larders, as before,
        As God decreed.

But walking 'neath those dappled-oak boughs
    Swishing along thro' crisp, crunching leaves,
Those silv'ry slend'rous birches, to earth endow,
    The plenteous benefit She needs to receive,
As our scurrying steps go scuffling along,
    We can already hear Spring's sweet song,
        And patiently await.

Soon the slumb'ring giants, their mantle shed,
  Will welcome the respite, and renew again,
Their lovely, oaken branches to rise from the dead,
  And refresh huge limbs in the sun and the rain,
To replenish the earth with nature's swift bounty,
  In the woods and fields of every English county,
    We love so well.

* * *

The Heavenly Brew

Fur of a fluffy rabbit
In the pot you must lay it,
Feather of bird and paw of cat,
The softness of a welcome mat,
Robin's chest and angel's wings,
The 'dawn chorus' songbirds sing,
For a charm of divine flings,
In the pot you must put these things.

———

Double, double gentle and kind,
In the pot you must stir, not grind!

Ben Yeardye
(aged 13)

Auschwitz
(Written after our visit to Poland, August 2002)

Through those hellish gates, walked a nation,
Sorrowing, woebegone Jews, for whom Israel pined,
Succumbing to a terrible predation,
Tremblingly-led in straggling lines,
 What had you done to earn this fate,
 Entering, crossing over, into a world of hate?

Falteringly, your minds in turmoil and confusion,
Little children clinging to their Jewish mothers,
The menfolk packed off, herded elsewhere, in exclusion,
Total bewilderment, as you helped one another,
 Along the road to freezing cattlesheds,
 Forced to lie on cold, hard bunk-beds.

How could you have known what was in store?
Bearing your possessions in battered cases and bags,
Your chamber-pots, metal utensils taken for 'their' war,
Clothing and items you revered, stolen, Jews reduced to rags,
 What inhumanity and indignity were yours,
 God alone knows the suffering you bore.

We witnessed all your deprivations, felt your tears,
Saw the long lines of concrete, lavatorial holes,
They will be there, to remain, for endless years,
A constant reminder of many thousand poor souls,
 Who, achingly, had any complained,
 Faced the mortal blows on them rained.

Our heartstrings tugged, and emotions running high,
To see little garments a child had once worn,
Knit by hand, with love, those mothers grieve and sigh,
Sorrowing for babies, hated and dying, cold by morn,
 Monstrous, 'they' purloined all you owned,
 And the gas-chambers, fed, moaned and groaned.

They had taken your hair, your teeth, your skin,
Many – so many – tortured, gassed, shot and hung,
Man's inhumanity to man, his greatest sin.
A testament to the world, and, though you have no tongue,
    Yet shall we, the masses, bear witness forever,
    To the sorrows of Auschwitz – and Jewish endeavour.

      We shall feel your presence evermore,
      Your surrounding spirits always restore,
        Then, in the name of God, sleep.

Suffolk Skies, in Autumn

Stretching as far as the eye can see,
Far away beyond the horizons of the mind,
The clamouring bells ring out joyously,
As ancient churches greet their own kind,
Their tall spires proclaim a faith so deep,
Each Sunday morning they call to their own,
From farmstead, town and village, a vigil to keep,
And give thanks to our Lord, for all He has done.

Over the broad sweep of harvested fields,
Scudding rainclouds dissolve away
From Suffolk lands, all ploughed and tilled,
As blue, sun-kissed skies again hold sway,
And a golden glow emanates behind dark clouds,
Casting rays of sunlight on rich brown soil,
Returning to a sombre, glowering mass of shrouds,
In one instant, the landscape to embroil.

The eerie whiteness of the broad evening sky,
Seen through the branches of stark, black trees,
Altering to blue beribboned wisps as the clouds vie
With golden sunbursts, and a wafting breeze
Stirs bronzed-gold ferns and cause red-russet leaves
To fall achingly down, aimlessly gathering to die
Until they fade, then to the muddy clods will cleave,
Enriching the rolling acreage, under an ever-changing sky.

An English Country Lane in Spring

To this most gracious setting, I found my lonely way,
And in this secret corner of old England, alive and well,
The sweet-smelling blossoms eased my trying day,
As I followed the tinkling sound of the old church bell.
    The early daffodils, waving in a light breeze,
    Moved my aching heart; brought their ease.

The dripping leaves hung low down from early showers,
As I made my lone way to an ancient Saxon church,
Nestling at the lane's end, mid bright Spring flowers,
Surrounded by yews, shimmering aspens and silver birch,
    Spring rain, replenishing the earth, to begin anew,
    After the harsh winter months, long overdue.

The urgency of budding plants, a new freshness in the air
The bright, uplifting greenery of ageless hedgerows,
Where little furry creatures scarper from the sun's glare,
'Midst primroses, wood anemones and sweet briar rose,
    Where the muddy tracks of an overgrown pathway,
    Led up to a tiny cottage, calling to me that day.

Surrounded, in isolation, by crab-apple trees,
Their pretty pink florets dazzling amongst haws and sloes,
Amid creeping blackberries, recovering from winter freeze,
This tiny place welcomed me, at the day's close,
    And I had come home, at last to find rest,
    Away from my anxieties and a troubled breast.

I had passed many old cottages, thatched and timeworn,
With their overhanging trees, and quaint garden's delight,
Where friendship awaited, and I could not be forlorn.
In this glowing haven, windswept skies shone bright,
    And a miraculous renewal had given me a pillow,
    By a gurgling stream, with graceful sweeping willow.

Your Nightmare, Their Delusion

He, the caddish rake! causing your anxiety and great pain,
She, the rampant witch! rising from the ashes, like a Phoenix,
   Stabbing you repeatedly, again and yet again,
   Their clandestine meetings driving you insane,
      Can they both ever hope to justify,
      Or maybe find a less sinful code to live by?
      Now they have gotten their own way,
      How will they live, day by day?

Will their troubled souls ever find some release,
Or can they simply walk away from unhappy minds?
   Will they ever find a certain peace,
   Turn lust to lifelong harmony; can inner guilt cease?
      Constantly reminded of the plunder,
      When young families they split asunder,
      It is certain no one else will they please,
      How can they ever find heart's ease?

Cheating on both of their former loved ones,
And breaking every precious, sacred marriage vow,
   To whom can they ever turn for help now?
   For no sympathy can their fellows endow!
      Life may yet deal cruel blows,
      To those who think they have no foes,
      Whom, to others, have caused tremendous pain,
      They might never find true peace again.

      Your nightmare will now become theirs,
    But you have the pride and endurance to forbear,
      Put yourself today, in God's loving care,
       And He will guide you through,
        Setting your course anew.

The Young Pilot
(For Battle of Britain Day, September 15th)

What were your last thoughts
    As you strode out to war?
Taking leave of your loved ones,
    Whose aching hearts you bore,
The local train that sped you away,
    Your destiny to await,
As they kissed, and hugged, and clung to you,
    With no insight as to your fate,
The last vision you had of them,
    Their small figures soon to disappear,
Pinched, anxious, worry-lined faces,
    Trying so hard to hide their tears.

Leaving your home-life far behind,
    Bravely setting out for the new,
Your young thoughts cling to romantic dreams,
    Yet to England's rescue you flew,
Aged only 18, you and others, answered the call,
    And mastered your art, to a Merlin's whirr,
In a few short weeks, a pilot emerged,
    Guiding a Super machine, to a steady purr,
High in the blue, it soared on a stealthy course,
    The pride of the nation resting on <u>you</u>,
Hurrah! Three cheers! Your very first hit,
    Many others to follow – all in your view!

Young man, your duty done,
    May you rest in peace with the Lord,
For your aircraft never returned to base,
    And you had to lay down your sword,
But we will remember your sacrifice,
    In the hour of glory – may this suffice.

This Land of Contrasts

The flatlands of Poland, we travelled through,
Their contrasting shades of many a hue,
With fields of maize and sweetcorn,
And golden rod, the wastelands adorn,
Men, with scythes, cut late summer grass,
For women and children, the stacks to amass.
      Before harsh winter, animal feed
      Must be gathered soon, for their need.

Neat hay-rolls tell of the summer yield,
Old farm implements at work in the field,
Storks leave high chimney nests to feed,
On succulent golden corn's fallen seed,
Ruddy brown horses pull ancient farmcarts,
From age-old farms, the workers depart
And traverse the well-worn country tracks,
Carting produce and sweet mown hay back,
      In good time, ere winter's storms,
      Cause deeply-piled snow to form.

Tall pines and silver birch trees lead the way
To the Tatra mountains, where we shall stay,
In pretty Zakopane, the skiers resort,
Where many an ancestral craft is wrought,
Passing distant globular churches, as decreed,
Long ago fashioned for the Slavic need,
In Wroclaw we found Gothic cathedral spires
And medieval gas-lamps, the city still fires,
      All of 92 lit morning and night,
      Around this timeless church, of the light.

In Kracow, the magical night-time square,
Teemed with colourful people, everywhere,
And a bugler played, upon each hour,
From the lofty pinnacle of an old church tower,
This hallowed place, where Kings were crowned,
And 16th century Copernicus 'capped and gowned',
The three-steepled cathedral of St. Sigismund,
Standing so tall and dignified on high ground,
  Its bells used only on the occasion,
  As when Pope John-Paul receives ovation.

Our visit to the Wieliczka salt mines,
Will long remind us of much harder times,
Then, floating downriver, on the Dunajec,
On three rafts slung together and held in check
By two young Poles so colourfully dressed,
As were dancers and musicians who sang at our behest!
Poland's bright, wild flowers and tethered cows,
Free range hens, wooden churches, old ploughs,
  Castles, and a turbulent history,
  All contribute to her air of mystery.

Gardening in the Rain

At daybreak, clear and bright, so much to be done,
  At the year's end, those lingering garden chores
Present a challenge, both in rain, or weakening sun,
  And as you answer the call of the great outdoors,
      Trying hard to beat the failing light in the end,
      On your indomitable spirit you must depend!

So when overcast skies make your heart sink fast,
  Rushing to and from the greenhouse, in a light drizzle,
The lawns cannot be mown, so nail your pride to the mast,
  When that sputtering bonfire ends in a sizzle,
      The rest of that hoeing will now have to wait,
      As reality dawns, today's rain will _not_ abate!

You need one extra hour, and, soaked to your skin,
  Wield secateurs with wet hands, pruning overgrown shrubs,
Hastily cutting and reducing dead wood to the bin,
  No need now, to fill watering-cans for flower tubs,
      It's soggy underfoot, squishy lawns, all a-dripping,
      Gardening in the rain, how simply ripping!

The ground, lightly forked over at start of day,
  Now shows small potholes; water-filled solid soil,
Can no longer be worked, it's as heavy as clay,
  Saturated to the skin and burdened from your toil,
      You call it a day and hasten to your lunch,
      But first, those sparkling chrysanths, hurried bunch!

Now rushing to hide tools away, slip-sliding as you go,
  The once steady rain increasing to a deluge, as you flee,
Retiring to your kitchen warmth, sparkling droplets aglow
  On the red-berried holly's glinting leaves, a robin, in glee,
    As you briskly rub down and dry out, hops to the ground
    And tweets his thanks for the luscious fare he found!

No Hiding Place

When you run away from reality, at those sad times,
    And you find there is no hiding place, anywhere,
You may have found somewhere new, in happier climes,
    Yet your mind constantly reminds that you care.

You may have escaped and made your fresh start,
    And realised that, at last, you are now free,
But still you can never avoid your aching heart,
    From whence you came, you may truly long to be.

You are on the run, not facing up to life's knocks,
    Leaving loved ones far behind, puzzled and forlorn.
Who, had you delved deeper, might have been your rocks,
    If you had only sought help, for an emerging new dawn.

Running away from truths is not the answer at all,
    For Conscience plays tricks, she follows wheresoe'er you go,
If you imagine you'll escape her, you're heading for a fall,
    She is ever at your shoulder, especially when you're low.

You must stand firm and bravely stand your ground,
    For troubles shared are troubles halved, so they say,
Face up to the reality of life, even when low down,
    And never imagine, for happiness, you need to run away.

So come home, when you're ready, to find us all there,
    Waiting, with strong shoulders, to lift you up high,
Give us the chance to show how much we care,
    To be there and carry your burdens, help is always nigh.

Melanie's Menagerie – at Hitcham

Bright morning breaks the bonds of night
    And peacock prepares himself for flight,
Surveying his kingdom above the branches high,
    From withered old tree he soon will fly,
Long since dead, at Hitcham Mill, o'er the pond,
    Giving night's refuge, for which he is fond,
His fellow sleeps on, gorgeous tail hangs down,
    Fanning turquoise feathers, both fawn and brown,
      Then emitting weird cries – as each flies!

The old white goose honks her delight,
    As a flurry of ducks descend from a height,
To land with a splash! making pretty swirls,
    Disturbing the pond into spreading whirls,
And little black moorhens, heads a-bobbing,
    Scurry hither and thither, to hidden nests a-jobbing,
Carrying twigs and debris to a 'missus' hatching eggs,
    Ignoring the ducks, pedalling fast little legs!
      To secret places – each one races!

Have you ever seen a duck climb a tree?
    Well, she did – to keep the peacocks company!
Then she took flight, fancying her chances
    With handsome Mr. Drake's amorous advances!
But the fickle fellow drove them all 'quackers',
    Fancying two white ladies, who fled to alpacas –
Docile creatures, creamy and sweet, sensing harm,
    Aimed noxious spittle to keep them all calm,
For their babies are due this coming Spring,
      They stake their claim – in the frame!

Here once more, seeing Melanie's menagerie again,
  Though suffering stress – all dulled our pain,
Visions of life, by midweek, cleared, made sense,
  Making pathways ahead seem far less dense!
These happiest of creatures she tends so well,
  Brought balm and contentment – clear as a bell,
To us both, in our GOLDEN ANNIVERSARY year –
  And we can return, enriched, to ones held dear,
  Holding fast to the rein and begin again.

* * *

Forward Together on Our Anniversary

Although, on earth's plane, tender
                memories may fade,
I pray we may recapture them in
                God's heavenly paradise,
As we wander, hand in hand, through some
                leafy woodland glade,
And reflect awhile that our happiest times
                will always be suffice
  To see us through to Eternity.

True love, they say, grows deeper with
                the passing of the years,
And we had found contentment and joy
                in so many, many ways,
Filling our hearts with happiness, but also
                sadness and some tears,
Yet always restoring them, with love, the
                happiness of our golden days,
  To carry us forward, heaven-bound.

Winter's Chill

In bleak January, all around lies bare,
     Neither hint of warmth, nor joy, anywhere,
And the frosted, lifeless, hardened earth,
     So despoiled by nature's heartless mirth,
For then, no spade, hard clods will turn
     And for warmer climes the heart doth yearn,
When the harsh month's chill is in the air,
     In parks and gardens, no portrayal of life there,
And a long cruel winter still reigns supreme,
     Thoughts of summertime remain a dream.

Never does any month seem so long,
     When even the brave robin shortens his song,
Stark January chilliness fills the brisk air,
     For greyness and despondency creep unaware
Upon the muted, tortured, glacial scene,
     And little woodland creatures no harvest glean
Until a melting earth reveals its seed-store,
     When they thankfully search the forest floor,
As a weakened sun permeates branches high,
     Soon to retreat in a dark, lowering sky.

And January gloom soon descends again,
     When angry snowstorms will cover the plain,
Pure whiteness falls on trees, shrubs and fields,
     Where little shelter for bird or beast yields,
Yet workers needs must to their places go,
     Despite the treachery or depth of the snow,
For others rely on these valiant, trusty fellows,
     Who pray the hardest month soon mellows,
Bringing in February's promise of early spring,
     When crocus, snowdrops, recovering earth sing.

And so, look to the future, a brand new dawn,
When sombre things fade, a newness reborn,
Only believing a richer pattern will emerge,
That wondrous life-givers still flourish and burge,
Just as you thought chance had no hope at all
And all your dreams were heading for a fall,
A sudden burst of joyful brilliance and light,
Eventually can change to bright day, from night,
And, as January fades, soon to haply disappear,
Take heart, enter upon a happier new year.

Then let those visions spring to life again,
Doing your best to forget sorrow and pain,
Positive thoughts can dispel gloom and fear,
When heartening deeds envisage great cheer,
Bring to mind our Lord's deep purpose for life,
He will not allow too much sorrow and strife,
Guiding you on to believe that He cares,
When January fades and Spring creeps unawares
Upon an enlightened scene; the golden light
Can restore your mind, bringing fresh new sight.

Be Thankful

When you next feel you're hard done by,
And nothing good is in sight at all,
That no one really cares if you live or die,
Stop and look around at your own 'marbled hall',
      Where you have all that anyone could need,
      To crave for any more – pure, selfish greed.

We, who have so much, cannot truly know
The suffering of others, in this harsh world
Your pampered lifestyle, and mine, always, ever so,
We have become grudging, miserly, churled,
      Forgetting the plight of others, in foreign lands,
      Believing them all to bedevil their clans.

Just look around your room, you have many,
All filled to capacity with treasured possessions,
Then think of the millions, who haven't any,
And remember, God's love for them swells, never lessens,
      The things you own are only there,
      Because you occupy Dame Fortune's chair!

When you take your family out for the day,
To a succulent lunch, a place of bonhomie, good cheer,
And revel in the niceties, any worries to allay,
Do you pause to reflect on the little child's tears?
      She has not eaten for days, her mother is dead
      Her siblings orphaned too, there is great dread.

She can only pray that kind neighbour's befriend,
When you can buy whole vases of pretty flowers
The only hope that she has, on them to depend,
Is for a handful of grain and to pray for showers
      Flowers are inedible and cannot be eaten,
      This little black child is surely beaten!

She will never know true mother love again,
Her father has disappeared, she knows not where,
Resigning herself, in her new role, to a sea of pain,
She must somehow care for her family, help them bear
       The anguish in young lives, hunger and thirst,
       A 12 year-old can never again put herself first.

And then she will face the ravages of Aids,
To follow rape when – oh! so very young,
Adding another little one to the fold; so afraid
That she will die and leave them all – among
       The clutches of the heartless, the uncaring ones,
       No choice, she resigns herself to whatever comes.

The Crucifix

You alone know, Lord, how deeply I weep,
  As though you were _my_ beloved son,
Each time I see a Crucifix, my tears you keep,
  I can feel your mortifying pain – yet have _none_,
        My eyes so readily fill, to overflow,
        Thoughts of your suffering bring deep woe.

I am too unworthy to kneel at your feet,
  Yet you died that I might repent and live,
When at last I found you, my life to complete,
  How can you, my Lord, my awesome sins forgive,
        That I may, one day, die in peace,
        Before my unhappy soul's release?

When, at church, though others may not see,
  My downcast head, my useless contrite tears,
I weep to recall that the folly of man's cruelty
  Set you hanging there, can sense your fears,
        As your dear mother, for her lonely son wept,
        And, at your feet, a silent vigil kept.

As they drove you through Jerusalem streets,
  The heavy cross, your burden, so severely borne,
Wearing a crown of thorns – how many heartbeats
  Away from Calvary, the hammered nails of scorn,
        For you, dear Lord Jesus, the crucified,
        Our Saviour, whose goodness was denied?

Through misted eyes, your sorrowing features I seek
  Yet cannot see for the heaviness in my heart,
Sensing bravery, courage, the soul of one so meek,
  So mild of manner, from all others set apart,
        And still I feel your loving arms surround me,
        Your comfort, kindness, beautiful face I see.

And I, so deeply aware of your suffering and pain,
  Abide in your goodness, ever to stay in your debt,
Will always be reminded of your anguish, again and again,
  Of the sacrifice made for me, and can never forget,
        The meaning of the Crucifix to me; the tears
        To remain throughout the coming years.

* * *

Grief

        When your grief is much too deep,
Too shattering for the spirit – too much to bear,
        It takes hold of your soul, you can only weep,
Then turn to the Lord – He is always there.
        And he alone will heal and save.

        We cannot begin to imagine another's grief,
We can only witness their anger and sad distress,
        Offering our sympathy, support and belief,
Whose loved ones, departed, He will gather, to bless,
        For He alone can heal and save.

        Thro' grief, you become an empty shell
And on-going life, seems to be, just a living Hell,
        But He comes – to heal and save.

Sunnier Climes

At Dawlish we had entered a different sphere
Where the heady air, so warm and so clear,
Pervaded our senses, relaxed our stiff frames,
Affording such pleasure as each heart claims,
When, ill-at-ease, sorely-wounded, woes so deep,
Shattered by circumstance, unable to sleep,
Overcome by depression, much sadness and fear,
Seeking respite in this "Golden Anniversary" year,
Here, in this tranquil corner of Devon,
Finding sweetness, the surety of heaven.

As we walked to Red Rocks, gulls screamed harshly
And we sat on a wall o'erlooking a placid sea,
Reminders of childhood days, Ramsgate's salty air,
Then pre-war Margate's quietude, a homely flair,
Still found here, in Devon, a sense of wellbeing to renew,
To dispel all anxieties, fresh spirit to imbue
As little bright trains to the Warren hurtled past,
With much noise and haste, each issued a blast,
And we sat in the sun sipping tea,
Discussing wildlife with locals, joyfully!

Thro' Beer's main street, rushing streams flow down,
Their outlet, the quaint harbour, below village ground,
Where fishing-boats assemble, await a master's hand,
To pursue the age-old seaman's craft, catches to land!
At Berry Head, the ancient fort, languished in warm sun
And we sat, ruminating, life's work nearly done,
Looking at The Channel; the guillemots, fulmars and gull
Will still be there when we are gone, life is never dull!
And, at Dawlish, we found a new way,
Such blessèd relief – to close our day.

We shall return, refreshed, our lives to simply renew
With so many precious things still left to do.

This Idyllic Place

I sat and watched an active tiny bee,
    Hard at work, on miniscule florets,
Busily extracting the bright pollen,
    In the tranquil, gracious harmony,
Of a beautiful lakeside setting,
    Surrounded by the luscious greenery
Of a late English summertime,
    This little creature ably vetting
Each pretty, small, mauve clover,
    As befitted its hardworking nature,
Finding contentment in its humble role,
    Oh, to find this much joy, in my soul!

Yet, as I surveyed its busy prancing,
    From one sweet flower, to another,
I realised we, each of us, had a part to play –
    And it set my heavy heart a-dancing,
Triumphantly, thro' God's almighty plan,
    And all my cares slowly, steadily lifted.
Amid the tranquillity of this peaceful scene,
    As I contemplated how it all began,
In the immensity and power of the universe,
    And for all its hurried endeavour and activity,
I could clearly see, that this one tiny bee,
    Was no more, no less, important than me.

As he carried out his little trade,
    Busily industrious all the day long,
In this beauteous world God made,
    My heart erupted, with joyous song.

The Welsh Marches, in Springtime

All around us, the reddened landscape sped past,
  Intermingled by fresh green fields, sweetly renewed,
The life-giving rain, dripping, from heavens o'ercast,
  A hidden sun sends golden warmth to earth, imbued
Upon the bright yellow, glowing joy of oil-seed rape,
  So intensely that each needs to avert their gaze
To secretly scan lustrous fast-moving cloud-shapes,
  Hovering, floating on by, to reveal a sudden solar blaze,
        To cover th'awakening with well-being again.

The newly-planted soil already shows tender shoots,
  Nurtured unfailingly by the Great Provider's hand.
And floriating goodness will emerge from scattered roots,
  When God's tool, the farmer, tills his soil, as planned,
Allowing hedgerow dividers to remain in their place,
  He hurriedly repairs the sweeping low stone walls,
Fringing aromatic pastures where wild flowers creep apace,
  The hardworking man answers his Maker's calls
        To wisely nourish the earth, as God's planner.

For St. George's Day, profusions of bright dandelions glow,
  Beneath early creamy-white hawthorns, laden with may,
And high crow's nests jostle large globules of mistletoe,
  Too hard for us to reach and there they must stay!
But we can touch pink-tinged horse chestnut racemes,
  As they point skywards and dance divinely in the trees,
Rejoicing in the overall warmth of the sun's beams,
  Spreading o'er the marches, tinged by a chill breeze,
        And all around us, God's love surrounds.

Swift clouds crossing the sun, cause shadows to speed by,
  Illuminating the horizon in various lilac-blue shades.
Sedate riverside willows given an unearthly glow, are nigh,
  Almond and cherry trees, whose sweet-smelling clusters pervade
The senses, and mating birds in heavily-hung wisteria dance
  And call their song, as cowslips with daffodils shyly cling
Below the quickthorn's pristine white blossoms, which prance
  With laburnum blooms and orange broom, as birds sing
    An evening lullaby, in umbrous splendour.

My Dedication, for You

At the end of the day, whatever shall I do,
     When I can no longer come home to you,
And your deserted place, a favourite armchair,
     No longer finds you sitting there,
Tell me, with our little bantering moments gone,
     Who else would I find to lean upon?

And can you cross your heart and readily say,
     You'd never miss me at the end of the day,
When the darkness of night closes in,
     To realise, on earth's plane, we can never meet again,
And will it all prove too much to bear,
     As you sit, all alone, in that same armchair?

I do confess, my life may come to an end,
     If, on your shoulders, I no longer depend,
For they were broad and brought me strength,
     When banishing those angry words we never meant,
And life, it seemed then, at its lowest ebb,
     Casting deep shadows around us, like a web.

Yet we always sailed right through it all,
     When our happiest moments we'd soon recall,
Of our children's troubles we tried to make sense,
     Sorting problems together, thro' tangles so dense,
We thought no solution could unravel each scene,
     And I often prayed to God, on Him to lean!

But you were always there too, to cradle my fall,
     And dedicated your life, to answer my call,
So now I can say, after all these many years,
     I know they brought great happiness, sometimes tears,
And to you, my best love, I give this standing ovation,
     For you have truly been my lifetime's dedication.